IMAGES
of America

FRASER

This early view of Fraser was taken from the second story of Steffens Hall, on the northwest corner of Utica Road and Fourteen Mile Road, looking south down Utica Street. (Courtesy of the Fraser Historical Society.)

ON THE COVER: The Fraser Lions Club's July parade has long been a favorite event in Fraser. The parade always has floats, clowns, politicians, organizations, animals, candy, and all the other ingredients that make up a small-town parade, including fireworks in the evening. (Courtesy of the Fraser Historical Society.)

IMAGES
of America

FRASER

Linda S. Champion, James Chamberlin,
Jan Dolland, Nancy Ehrke, Alan Naldrett,
Gary Nizio, and Marilynn D. Wright
for the Fraser Historical Society

ARCADIA
PUBLISHING

Published by Arcadia Publishing
Charleston, South Carolina

Library of Congress Control Number: 2013931974

For all general information, please contact Arcadia Publishing:
Telephone 843-853-2070
Fax 843-853-0044
E-mail sales@arcadiapublishing.com
For customer service and orders:
Toll-Free 1-888-313-2665

Visit us on the Internet at www.arcadiapublishing.com

*This book is dedicated to the pioneers who built Fraser, including
Alexander D. Fraser; the Baumgartner, Eberlein, Reindel,
Schott, and Steffens families; and everyone who sacrificed
to build the Fraser settlement into the city it is today.*

CONTENTS

ACKNOWLEDGMENTS

Unless otherwise noted, all photographs appear courtesy of the Fraser Historical Society. We, the authors, would like to thank Lori Bargowski for tech help, Kay M. Champion for proofreading, Linda Champion, the late Diana L. Lang, and the original commissioners and society members who spent endless hours requesting, gathering, numbering, indexing, captioning, and organizing Fraser's historic photographs, including Marilyn Jennings, Gini Messier, Frank Clark, Charlotte Maier, Mary Steffans, Mike Foster, Dave Keown, and everyone else who donated photos. We are sorry for the ones we missed. Your work has proved invaluable to the authors. We also thank Robert Brannon, Vince Calabrese, David A. Castle, Gail M. Zabowski, Lynn Lyon, Sandy Decker, and all the citizens of Fraser who made history and gave us such good material to work with.

Images of America: *Fraser* was written by the following authors:

Chapter One: The Baumgartner Family by Linda S. Champion

Chapter Two: Early Residents and Homes by Jan Dolland

Chapter Three: Government and Military by Nancy Ehrke and Gary Nizio

Chapter Four: Transportation by Gary Nizio, Nancy Ehrke, and Alan Naldrett

Chapter Five: Farms and Farm Views by James Chamberlin

Chapter Six: Religion and Education by Alan Naldrett

Chapter Seven: Clubs and Organizations by Marilynn D. Wright

Chapter Eight: Business and Industry by Linda S. Champion

Chapter Nine: Leisure and Recreation by Linda S. Champion

INTRODUCTION

The history of Fraser began in 1838 when founder Alexander D. Fraser established the village near the Chicago, Detroit & Canada Grand Trunk Junction Railroad Company station, at the intersection of Detroit and Utica Plank Roads, in south central Macomb County. The Utica Plank Road was established in 1851, when the Detroit Erin Blank Road Company was built off the Gratiot Turnpike to go to the city of Utica.

The railroad station was built on Depot Road, which is still called that today. To take advantage of the commercial prospects of the train going through the area, prominent Detroit lawyer Alexander D. Fraser bought land near the depot in 1838 and platted a village. He also reputedly built and operated a hotel in the area. He sold parts of the land throughout the 1860s until 1870; by that time, he was apparently no longer residing in the village. He drowned in Detroit in 1871 after a distinguished legal career, and the new village was named for him. Fraser comes from the old French word *fraise* (strawberry), which is why the Fraser Historical Society's newsletter is named *Strawberry Preserves*.

Many of the first settlers were of German descent. Fred Eberlein built the first business, a blacksmith shop, in 1856. In 1865, he built a stave mill.

In 1860, the growing area opened a post office with Leonard Scott as the first postmaster. Later, in 1860, James McPherson became the postmaster, and the area was referred to as McPhersonville. In 1863, the name was changed back to Fraser.

In 1894, when Fraser was incorporated as a village by the Michigan state legislature, the spelling was listed with a "z." Throughout the early histories of Fraser, it is spelled both Fraser and Frazer. The two spellings, even for Alexander D. Fraser, appear to be interchangeable throughout the years until 1928, when a vote was finally enacted to establish the spelling as Fraser.

The new village had a population of 230, and its businesses included the post office, a town hall, a blacksmith shop, the stave mill, a cigar manufacturer, the depot, a hotel, school, Lutheran church, and several other stores.

In 1905, a fire that started at Fourteen Mile and Utica Roads destroyed many of the town buildings.

The State Bank of Fraser was established in 1910, and in 1930, a majestic building was built at the same Fourteen Mile and Utica Roads intersection.

In the 1920s, Fraser continued to grow as many people of Belgian descent moved into the area. In 1928, it was proposed by Walter C. Steffens, village president and member of the County Plat Board, that a highway be constructed. This was later named Groesbeck Highway, after Alexander Groesbeck, the first and only Macomb County governor of Michigan to date. The construction of Groesbeck Highway contributed greatly to the growth of Fraser.

Although Fraser had slow growth at first (its population was still only 747 in 1940), by 1956, the population had ballooned to 3,363, making it large enough to be chartered as a city. In anticipation of this, Fraser annexed one square mile of Erin Township. The village had previously annexed an area near Fourteen Mile and Garfield Roads and established the Municipal Park in 1940. This increased the total area of Fraser to four square miles.

In December 1956 a city charter was approved, and in January 1957, the city of Fraser was officially established. During the 1960s, Fraser grew by 68 percent to become a thriving community.

Today, Fraser has many amenities, including its own police and fire departments, good infrastructure, and a prosperous economy.

This image from 1928 shows the Fraser Motor Company, which was an Oldsmobile dealership.

One

THE BAUMGARTNER FAMILY

John Christian Baumgartner (1828–1905) and Samantha (Daniels) Baumgartner (1834–1892) married on October 12, 1856. He was born in Bavaria, Germany, on March 14, 1828, immigrated to the United States in 1852, and settled in Greenfield Township, Wayne County, Michigan, where he wed 22-year-old Samantha at age 28. She lived in Ohio. They were living in Greenfield Township when their first five sons were born. On February 15, 1856, John bought 80 acres that bordered on the roads of Masonic Boulevard and Kelly Road. The 1870 census shows the family was living in Erin Township with five sons, ages one to twelve years old. As the family grew, John built a larger two-story brick home on the corner of these two roads in 1875. This structure is now known as the Baumgartner House. At that time, he had six sons and one daughter; the last Baumgartner child, their second daughter, was born in 1876.

John Baumgartner built a large two-story brick home on his corner lot at Masonic Boulevard and Kelly Road. This structure is now known as the Baumgartner House. The Baumgartner House went through many different owners until it was purchased by the city of Fraser in 1981. In the 1940s, it was painted white. In 1982, it had a more modern look. Charles Baumgartner (1860–1947) held two patents and mined in Virginia until the time of his mother's death. He married Neva Daniels and had two sons, Gordon and Horace. In 1894, John C. (1863–1947) married Octavia Alphonsina "Allie" Peltier, whose great-grandfather's daughter was the mother of Alexander Fraser, the founder of Fraser. In 1860, David I. Baumgartner (1871–1911) sustained serious injuries in a building collapse at Detroit's Eastern Market, which also injured his mother. In 1905, after his father died, he moved into the Baumgartner family estate with his two sisters.

Samantha Baumgartner (above) preceded her husband John in death on December 24, 1892. The cause of death is listed as due to the injuries she incurred at the Eastern Market accident exactly two years before the date of her death. She had been there selling her apples, which people came from miles around to buy since they were so delicious. One couple who owned the house in the 1930s was Christian and Hilda Hoerling. Below, from left to right, Hilda, Charlotte Maier, and Alma Seitz are pictured in the side yard of the Baumgartner house. When John C. Baumgartner died, his personal estate was estimated at $4,000 and his real estate at $10,000. Because there was no will, his estate went into probate. A partial list of his possessions included a two-horse farm wagon, a white 22-year-old mare and a white 15-year-old gelding, two red cows, one buffalo robe, six fat hogs, one wheelbarrow, and other farm equipment, since that had been his primary occupation.

The first Baumgartner family to reside in the Baumgartner House is shown on a picnic on Belle Isle in Detroit. The historical society has restored the inside of the house to look as it did at the time this family resided in the mansion. Other generations that resided in the house are pictured below. The 80 acres of land that John Baumgartner bought in 1856 extended from Kelly Road to Groesbeck Highway and from Masonic Boulevard to Fourteen Mile Road. The area near the newly built house came to have two barns, a cowshed, a pigpen, and a smokehouse. Family members raised their own produce, and Samantha had the apple orchard. John purchased the original tract of land for $1,200. After his death at age 77, the house was auctioned off to son David. After the Baumgartners sold it to Orville and Ida Shattuck, it was then owned (for only a month) by Fred and Louise Dettmer in 1920. Other owners include Christian and Hilda Hoerling, Gottfried and Melanie Lambrecht in 1942, and John and Petronilla Huber in May 1945. The city of Fraser acquired the property from the Huber estate on August 24, 1981, for $62,000.

Baumgartner House was built in the German architectural style known as *Rundbogenstil*. The style included staircases, and it was common for families to take photographs in front of one of the staircases, as pictured here. This style was popular in Germany between 1840 and 1850, and many German immigrants copied it. To meet the standards of Rundbogenstil, a house must be brick, must be square or almost square (Baumgartner House is 32 by 22 feet), the windows must be round at the top, and the corbeling (an arrangement of bricks projecting from the face of the wall, generally for support) must be over and beneath the windows. Because of the brief period during which this style was popular, it is very rare.

There were many outbuildings on the Baumgartner farm. The smokehouse, pictured at left, was an important feature of farms at the turn of the 20th century. It was a building where meat was cured with smoke. This helped to preserve the food and give it flavor. The original barn is pictured below with Marjorie on the seat of the roller machine. Although not an original structure on the Baumgartners' property, the Hemme Barn was preserved and brought to the Baumgartner House since it is from the same era. When property on Mulvey Road was purchased for development, the Fraser Historical Commission approached the buyers about saving this 125-year-old barn. William and Mary Martin of Villas of Pine Ridge donated the Hemme Barn to the commission.

The Hemme Barn is named for Gotthold Hemme, born in Germany on September 7, 1822. He learned his trade and became a journeyman carpenter. He and his wife and daughter immigrated and eventually traveled to Michigan, living in Erin Township, Macomb County. In 1865, he bought 20 acres from John Priehs on Mulvey Road, which was then in Clinton Township. At this site, he built the barn. The Hemme farmhouse, which was the main house on the property where the Hemme Barn was originally located, was also owned by the Frohreip, Schoen, and Hewins families. This 1970s photograph of the house depicts a frame farmhouse typically built by German farmers of the late 1800s.

The Hemme Barn is one of the oldest intact barns in the area. It is pictured above in the mid-1970s, and below after being restored by the historical society. Gotthold Hemme built this barn during the Civil War. It was called a "double-door team barn," which provided a wider opening to drive a team of horses with a wagon inside. The barn is of notch-and-peg construction, and the boards are secured with square steel-cut nails. The main timbers are hand-hewn logs. German crosses are carved at the top on either side, possibly for ventilation or simply for decoration. Gotthold Hemme died on November 10, 1896, leaving this beautiful barn in wonderful condition. On December 8–9, 1990, nine members of the Fraser Lions Club tagged all the boards and beams of the Hemme Barn. Twenty-three Lions Club members dismantled the barn on December 15–16. After the hand-hewn timbers and boards were moved to the Baumgartner property, they sat until they were again moved to the city's Department of Public Works yard in 1992. This was the same year that Mike Stitt, a master barn raiser, agreed to take on the task of reassembling the barn.

Workers raised the barn on a cold, rainy Saturday in 1992. The hand-hewn timbers were notched and pegged as in days of yore and lifted by brute strength. The barn, now on the northwest side of the Baumgartner House, joins the Depot Visitor Center, which was added in 2007. The Depot Visitor Center houses the archives of the Fraser Historical Society.

One of the young sons of John Baumgartner is pictured at left standing on a chair inside the house. The many sons and daughters of John Baumgartner made for quite an extended family, as shown by the 1930s family photograph below outside the Baumgartner House.

Two

EARLY RESIDENTS AND HOMES

Frederick Reindel purchased a farm at the northwest corner of Masonic Boulevard and Utica Road after moving from Halfway, which is now Eastpointe. His son Charles established a hardware store, which, as of 2013, is still in existence and is operated by Charles's grandson, also named Charles.

Fred Schott's house is depicted in the idyllic winter scene above. Schott established a dry goods and grocery store on Utica Road, just south of Fourteen Mile Road. His son Alfred eventually took over the business. As it grew, the business moved to Fourteen Mile Road between Utica and Garfield Roads, as shown in the 1960s photograph below. Schott's Grocery Store still operates as of 2013.

August and Fredrika Frohreip purchased a 60-acre farm on Mulvey Road between Garfield and Utica Roads. Their son William took over the big farm, and August purchased Gotthold Hemme's 7.5-acre farm in 1895. In 1926, they sold the farm and moved to East Detroit, now Eastpointe.

Charles Knorr arrived in Fraser in 1866 and purchased the stave mill from Fred Eberlein. In 1875, he took Charles Steffens in as a partner. By 1888, the mill, pictured below, employed about 50 people, which made it one of the largest employers in the area.

Alexander James Fraser (1831–1871) established the village of Fraser in 1858. To take advantage of the train going through the area, he built and operated a hotel near the train station. By 1864, his lands had reverted back to the auditor general. He favored his father, Alexander David, whose likeness is shown here. His father outlived him by six years.

Frederick Eberlein came to Fraser in 1856 and was one of the biggest and strongest men in the area. He established the first store in Fraser, a blacksmith shop, on the corner of Utica and Fourteen Mile Roads. He opened a sawmill in 1865. Eberlein is pictured below with his wife celebrating his 80th birthday on July 12, 1915.

Three

GOVERNMENT AND MILITARY

In 1905, a fire started at Fourteen Mile and Utica Roads, destroying several stores and buildings in the area. These included a slaughterhouse, agricultural machinery building, bowling alley, meat market, cigar shop, tavern, public hall, and storage building. Seen standing on the rubble from the fire is Paul Soltman.

In 1938, the Fraser Post Office was a small building between Schneider Hardware (above) and Schott's Grocery Store. This location was next to the bank on Utica Road. In 1919, Fred Schott had a small post office building constructed next to his market on Utica Road. The first postmaster in this building was George Horany, who, after being appointed, operated a barbershop from the building. The building was bought and moved to Anita Street by the Reagen family. Schott's Grocery Store was originally called the Bloss & Schott General Store (below). Frederick Schott moved from Waldenburg, Michigan (near Twenty-two Mile Road and Romeo Plank Road) to Fraser. He bought the grocery and dry goods business from Charles Klien and took on William Bloss as a partner, later dissolving the partnership and taking on his brother Charles as his new partner.

In 1916, the saloon portion of Schott's business closed due to Prohibition. Fred sold the business to his son Alfred in 1930. Alfred was a founding member of the Fraser Chamber of Commerce, as well as a sponsor of youth leagues and sports. In 1971, Alfred sold the business to a new owner who went bankrupt. Taking the business back, he sold it in 1975, and since the Schott's Grocery Store name was included in the purchase, Schott's Grocery Store is still a major business of Fraser in 2013.

The water tower in Fraser was built in 1948 on Fourteen Mile Road on city property west of Utica Road. The tower was used until 1964, when Detroit water was pumped into Fraser, making the water tower obsolete. Planes taking off and landing from McKinley Airport quite often passed near the tower. The water tower was removed and sold to another community for $1 around 1973. The map, issued during Fraser's centennial in 1995, shows the city boundaries.

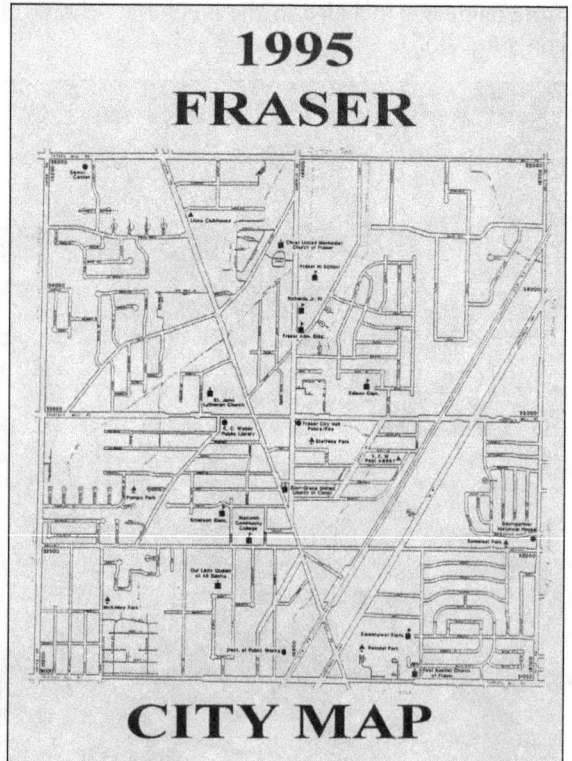

1995
FRASER

CITY MAP

In 1949, the Fraser firehouse had two trucks to fight fires with. Most of the firefighting staff was on call to help neighboring areas fight their fires also. Fraser would assist and be assisted by Roseville, Eastpointe, Warren, and other nearby municipalities. Fire protection was a serious subject since Fraser suffered major fires in 1905 and 1921. Until the 1970s, the firefighting equipment was stored near city hall.

The first home delivery of mail in Fraser began in 1958. In the early days, postmasters had a lot of pull with how an area was settled. An earlier name for Fraser was McPhersonville, after James McPherson, the postmaster. It was later changed back to Fraser.

In 1959, the old city hall was the storage place for the various vehicles used to maintain the city. In most towns, the municipal building was a common meeting place for the community and served many purposes, such as storing town vehicles and hosting civic events. At this time, the population of Fraser was approximately 3,400.

In November 1975, at the Fraser Town Hall, Mayor James J. Pompo swore Councilman Joseph F. Boris Jr. into office. Other councilmen sworn in that day were George Shepherd and Leonard Bassett. As a village, a president and council governed Fraser. As a city, the mayor is the chief town officer.

To celebrate an addition to the Fraser Library, there was a ground breaking ceremony in 1978. Those pictured are, from left to right: Walter H. Lang, John M. Clarkson, Mayor James J. Pompo, Loretta Hefka, Leonard E. Bassett, Nan Toger, Joseph F. Boris Jr., and Dr. D.H. Folkman. The library is located in the old schoolhouse of St. John Lutheran Church, and the new building addition was being constructed to expand it. The old school and new addition are being used as of 2013. The library's collection contains over 64,000 volumes and circulates over 126,000 items per year.

The old city hall is shown here. It was demolished to make room for the new city hall presently being used by the city of Fraser.

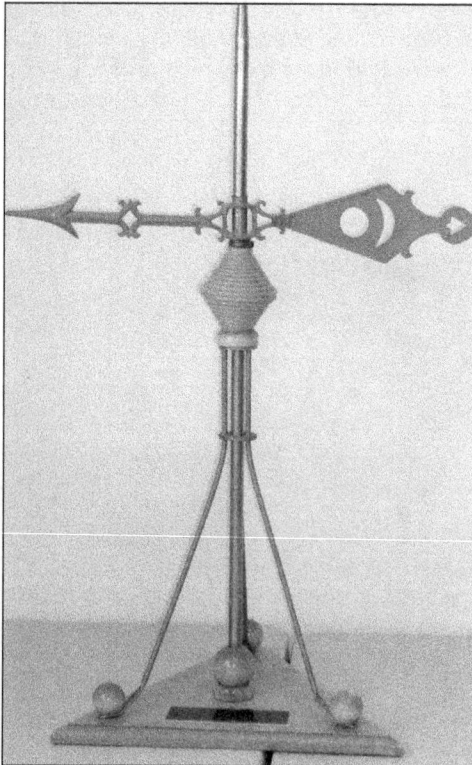

The historical commission wanted to preserve the weathervane that was on top of the cupola above the old city hall. Diane Lang and Bob Buffa were able to obtain the weathervane for the museum. Bob went to the Department of Public Works and brought the weathervane to the museum. Later, he took it home, cleaned it up, and restored it. He then mounted it on a platform of wood. He put a metal plaque on it, and it was ready to be displayed for the public. It is currently on display in the Depot Visitor Center at the site of the Baumgartner Museum as part of the collection of the Fraser Historical Society.

It was in the year 2000 when the Fraser City Hall was demolished to make room to build the new city hall. The mayor and city council have offices in the city hall, and council meetings are held there. It is a place where people with questions about city government can come and where residents can pay their taxes and go to city council meetings.

Besides the restoration of the Baumgartner House, another project of the Fraser Historical Society was the fence around the Pioneer Cemetery (above), which was established in 1864 and is behind the Fraser Public Library. The city hall (below) has since been a focal point for Fraser, with the park and athletic fields behind it. To keep the area green for the enjoyment of residents, Fraser has a number of parks. The oldest, biggest, and main one is Steffens Park, bordered by Fourteen Mile Road, Garfield Road, and Park Lane at the same site as the Fraser City Hall. It was dedicated in 1940 by a proclamation of the village council with trees planted to commemorate the event. It was named after 1963 to honor village president Walter C. Steffens; a monument was built to mark the occasion. Steffens was quite a part of the city's history, having been the village president when the land was purchased for a city park.

The City of Fraser Public Safety Honor Guard is pictured at rest after performing the World Trade Center Honor Flag Ceremony. To honor the flag that flew over the World Trade Center during the search and rescue and to honor the victims and first responders of the disaster, honor guards carried the flag at the closing of the event on September 18, 2001. (Both courtesy of Mike Carnagie and Vince Calabrese.)

One of the main functions of local government is to maintain access roads, as illustrated by the 1920 road crew on Utica Road near Reindel's Hardware. Utica Road had come a long way since it was pictured (below) in an illustration of the Fourteen Mile and Utica Roads area in an 1875 atlas.

Four

TRANSPORTATION

The Grand Trunk Railway system had the power to make or break a settlement. When Alexander D. Fraser read a notice that the railway would be passing through what would become Fraser, he bought land in the area and built the Fraser Hotel, present-day Ballew's Bar and Grill. The Grand Trunk Railway operated in Connecticut, Maine, Michigan, Massachusetts, New Hampshire, and Vermont, as well as the Canadian provinces of Ontario and Quebec.

HORSES, BUGGIES and DERBIES

Horse and buggy was an essential means of transportation before autos and the widespread use of trains, as demonstrated by Arthur Sieger and his family. Most mid-sized settlements of the 1890s, such as New Baltimore, Romeo, and Mount Clemens, had a carriage maker. Many carriage makers, such as the Fisher brothers, changed to producing chassis, frames, and other parts for automobiles. Above, Arthur Sieger in a horse-drawn buggy is a reminder of how big the carriage construction industry was before the advent of the automobile. August Fruehauf was a blacksmith and carriage maker from Fraser who grew up on Church Street, now named Fruehauf Avenue in his honor. He started making boat trailers in 1914 and, in 1918, incorporated as the Fruehauf Trailer Company, later to become the Fruehauf Trailer Corporation. The company coined the name "semi-trailer" and was one of the largest trailer producers in the world until 1997, when Wabash National Corporation purchased it. One of the classic Fruehauf trailer models, powered by a Kenworth cab, is pictured below.

Over the years, the roads and highways of Fraser have improved; note the differences between the early picture of Utica Road and the 1970 aerial shot of Fourteen Mile and Utica Roads.

Fraser's depot, built in 1858–1859, was located at the end of Depot Road on the east side of the tracks, as seen in 1960. It was built of brick, similar in architectural style to other Grand Trunk Railway depots built in Richmond, New Haven, Smiths Creek, Mount Clemens, and Port Huron. The depot was wired for electricity in 1926 and had an outhouse and hand pump until 1959, when inside facilities were installed. Young Thomas Edison worked on the train line and was a frequent visitor to Fraser. The Fraser Depot was demolished in approximately 1986. The Smiths Creek original depot is now at Greenfield Village, while the Mount Clemens Depot, where Edison saved the stationmaster's son from falling on the train tracks, still stands as of 2013 and is now the Michigan Transit Museum.

In Fraser, the track keeper had his own house near the depot. In the view of the tracks at Masonic Boulevard, looking toward Mount Clemens from the Fraser Depot, one can see the back of the Gideon House. When the original Grand Trunk Railway went through, Fraser was one of the original stops, which also included Detroit, Mount Clemens, New Haven, Richmond (Lenox), and Smiths Creek.

This is a rare 1908 Auto Wagon made by International Harvester, well-known makers of farm equipment. It was owned by Fraser hardware store proprietor Charlie Reindel. This was the only automobile he ever owned, and he lived for 97 years.

Perhaps impressed with the longevity of the vehicle, in 1991 Charlie Reindel's grandson, Charles, restored the International Harvester auto, which has so far made it to 2013. The International Harvester Co. was famous for tractors. Less well known was their truck series and even less well known was the Auto Wagon, which was first produced in the early 1900s.

One way to get an aerial view of Fraser was by taking a plane out of McKinley Airport, located on Utica Road. The airport was started by and named for Otis McKinley (1911–1994), a dentist from Detroit who moved to Fraser in 1938 and served as a councilman and mayor of Fraser. Otis McKinley, besides producing what the county agent proclaimed the "finest yield of corn in the county," took up flying in 1942 and bought a plane. His 40 acres of corn farmland shared its space with what became a landing strip.

The private airport was opened to the public in 1946 and expanded to 120 acres of elaborately drained and graded sod. Plane pilots would complain when they would not be allowed to use the 2,600-foot field in wet weather because Dr. McKinley, who did not want the sod to be ruined, forbade it. In the late 1940s, a new, 3,000-foot, all-weather landing strip that went east to west was added. The north-to-south strip remained sod. In 1950, a new 31-plane hangar was built. Called the McKinley Airport Administration Building, it contained the flight office for the McKinley Aircraft Company.

Group of Flight Instructors reading from left to right Mauno Nikander, Instrument Instructor, Walter Hulsberg, Flight Instructor, Arne Pelton, field C.A.A. Flight Examiner and Chief Pilot, Al Lamter, Flight Instructor, J. W. McCracken, Ground School Instructor.

Flying lessons could be taken at McKinley Airport. The airport had a large group of flight instructors, pictured here from left to right: Mauno Nikander, instrument instructor; Walter Hulsberg, flight instructor; Arne Pelton, field CAA flight examiner and chief pilot; Al Lamter, flight instructor; and J.W. McCracken, ground school instructor.

Five

FARMS AND FARM VIEWS

The William Klein farm is pictured on Utica Road, south of present-day Fifteen Mile Road. A close look shows what some observers believe to be the steeple of the old Buffalo Church, which would have been just north of the farm site.

FRASER

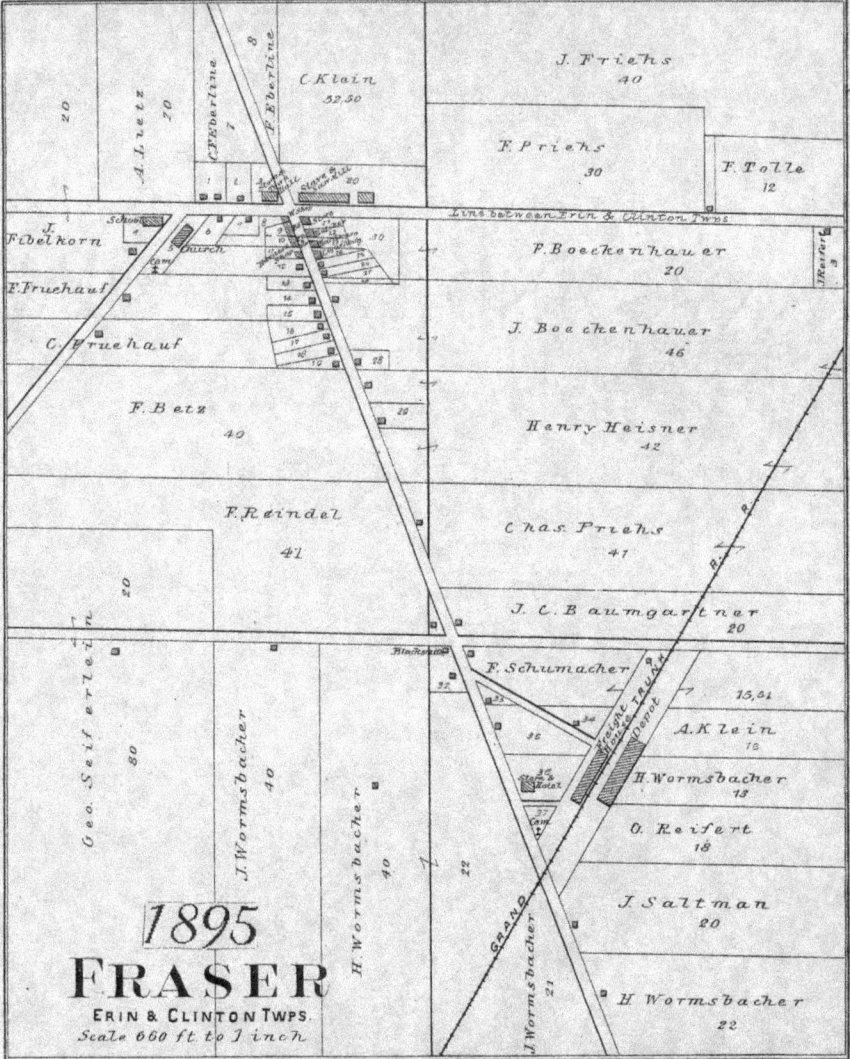

One of the earliest maps of Fraser since its incorporation as a village in 1894 is this one from 1895 that shows the village straddling two townships. The east-west road at the north end is present-day Fourteen Mile Road. Erin Township is to the south, and Clinton Township is to the north while the Fruehauf Farms are at the northwest boundary. The first Fruehauf trailer was built there in 1914. After building several more trailers to haul lumber and wood products for a local merchant, August Fruehauf incorporated his trailer manufacturing business in 1918 to form the Fruehauf Trailer Company.

Charles Steffens, father of George Steffens (pictured above), was the first president of the village when it was incorporated in 1894. George Steffens served as village president from 1915 to 1918. The new village had a population of 230 residents. The Steffens farm consisted of 145 acres on the east side of the village, between present-day Thirteen Mile Road and Masonic Boulevard, west of Kelly Road. It neighbored the Baumgartner Farm, which was north of Masonic Boulevard. The Steffens Sawmill is pictured below and was a major employer in Fraser for many years.

The Gottlieb Hemme Farm was on Mulvey Road in Northwest Fraser. The barn was built about 1865 and is probably one of the last, if not the oldest, standing "double-door team barns" in Macomb County. The barn was donated to the Fraser Historical Commission in 1988, dismantled in 1990, and moved offsite. Reconstruction on land behind the Baumgartner House was completed in 1994, where the barn still stands and is in use for many historical commission events.

Frederick Eberlein established a blacksmith shop, the first recorded business in Fraser, and lived on Utica Road in the pictured Sears, Roebuck & Company prefabricated farmhouse. He married Wilhelmina Klein, daughter of another Fraser founding family.

The Leitz farmhouse, part of the Fraser landscape from 1889 to 1996, was located at 33450 Klein Road, the site of the present-day Richards Junior High cafeteria. The Leitz farm was one of the last farms in the area. Fraser was a desirable location for farmers due to the proximity of the railroad and the local depot.

The John Schneider-Priehs-Lang house, named for the various owners, was a picturesque farmhouse on the outskirts of Fraser. As farm machinery became more sophisticated, it became easier to operate a farm with less people. As the Great Depression came, many of the smaller farms were incorporated into larger ones.

Edward Vermander, a 1912 graduate of Mount Clemens High School who studied business administration at Notre Dame's business school, owned the Vermander farm on Fifteen Mile Road. In 1912, anyone in Macomb County who graduated eighth grade in the one-room schoolhouses had to go to Mount Clemens for high school.

In 1939, Victor Puls, George Puls, Vic Puls, Ed Leitz, Ed Malow, Art Puls, Bill Ahrens, and Ed Pul's father take a break from threshing. Farmwork was never easy, but many hands made work lighter as neighbors helped each other out.

Six

RELIGION AND EDUCATION

The first schools of Fraser were parochial schools, which were used for the education of the children of the churchgoers. The first school in the Fraser area was constructed in 1852 and was the parochial school of the Buffalo Lutheran Church. Known as the Buffalo School, it was constructed next to the church. They were both located on Utica Road, about a quarter mile south of Fifteen Mile Road. The school was north of the church; both were frame buildings using wood cleared from the farmlands.

Other Fraser children would attend school in Erin Township, District No. 7. Erin Township was the neighboring area to Fraser that later grew into the city of Roseville. Settled by Irish Protestants, the original name was Orange Township.

The next school to be located in Fraser was the one belonging to St. John Lutheran Church. In 1864, 28 families left the Buffalo Lutheran Church and formed their own church, naming it St. John Lutheran Church. On February 22, 1864, St. John Lutheran School was founded on Fourteen Mile Road. The salary for the first teacher was $200 per year, with the use of a free house and free wood. Pictured are two early St. John Lutheran Schools. The building below is now the town library.

St. John Lutheran Church started the chief cemetery of Fraser on Mulvey Road at Fourteen Mile Road. Built around a hill, it is unique and is of beautiful quality. Pictured above is the Steffens mausoleum. The first burial was "Grandma Ahrens," who originally owned the property and wanted to be buried in her back garden.

The second school in the area was built in 1877 at Cady's Corner, a settlement at Moravian and Utica Roads near Fraser in Clinton Township. It had a US post office from 1864 until 1906. It was named for Chauncey G. Cady (1803–1893) who held many local offices, including township supervisor. From 1849 until 1857, he was a member of the Michigan state legislature. He was the Macomb County drain commissioner for many years and was the first president of the Pioneer Society, which is now the Macomb County Historical Society. He lived to be 90 and is interred in Clinton Grove Cemetery. A public schoolhouse was located at the corner of Canfield (now Thirteen Mile) and Utica Roads. Called Canfield School, it was built in 1888 for $2,000. The one-room frame schoolhouse was used until 1924, when fire destroyed it.

The Mulvey School (above) was located on Fifteen Mile Road between Utica and Garfield Roads around 1907 and was not far from Mulvey Road, the oldest road in Fraser. Mulvey Road was originally a Native American trail and has the curvy aspect of many Native American trails. Native Americans would make their trails go around bodies of water and large trees, as opposed to what 21st-century people do—build over or remove. The first brick school (below) was built in 1884 on Fourteen Mile Road, a block west of Utica Road. A two-story structure, it is now part of the E.C. Weber Fraser Public Library. Even though this school was much larger and more able to accommodate the educational needs of the Fraser community, there was still an overflow of students, and some were housed in the former parish hall.

Pictured are St. John Lutheran schoolchildren in the early 1900s. This building became the children's section of the E.C. Weber Fraser Public Library, named for a prominent pastor of St. John Lutheran Church.

Further growth necessitated another St. John Lutheran School to be erected in 1948. Many schoolhouses of this era were still of the one-room variety and were not consolidated into school districts. Parochial schools, such as the one at St. John Lutheran Church, were often the first in an area, and this was the case with Fraser. One-room schoolhouses would have one teacher teaching all the students in grades one through eight.

A six-room addition was added to the new St. John Lutheran School in 1957 and then a three-room addition in 1964. Most teachers will say that 25 students in a first-grade class are a bit too many. Imagine having 41 six-year-old students in a classroom at the same time!

Presently, the St. John Lutheran School is a victim of its own success. School enrollment is limited, and unfortunately, many prospective students have to be turned away. In 1945, the introduction of bus transportation allowed over 200 pupils daily to get to and from school. This school became too small in 1948, and a new one was built on the north side of Fourteen Mile Road. Pictured below is the dedication ceremony for the school.

A schoolhouse located at Sixteen Mile and Utica Roads was also destroyed by fire in 1924. Known as the Cady School, a new two-story brick building was constructed in 1927 and later became the Einstein Senior Center. In the 1920s, money raised through the sale of dog licenses was used to help finance the schools.

In 1924, Fraser Elementary and High School was built and housed kindergarten through the 12th grade. In 1958, a separate elementary school was built and opened in 1959. This school was at first named South-East Fraser School. In the 1970s many school names were changed to honor famous persons, and this school's name was changed to Dwight D. Eisenhower School (pictured). Kathy Graham, a teacher at Eisenhower Elementary School for many years, reminisces about being so crowded that they moved into the school before it was finished. She would chase workmen out of the classroom when it was time for school to start.

In 1958, the Cady School System merged with Fraser School District. In the early 1960s, due to a bond improvement issue passed by the city in 1959, Dr. Jonas A. Salk School was built on Fifteen Mile Road and served part of Fraser. As Fraser began a practice of naming schools for famous Americans, another school on Thirteen Mile Road and Grove Street (now known as Callahan) was named for Mark Twain, and a school built at Fourteen Mile and Garfield Roads was named for Thomas Edison. In 1956, the high school, which is present-day Howard C. Richards Junior High, was built. Pictured is Thomas Edison Elementary School.

Similar to South-East Fraser School changing its name to honor President Eisenhower, Fraser Elementary School changed its name to J.F. Kennedy High in 1964 to honor the US president who was assassinated the previous year. Kennedy Junior High was sold to Macomb County Community College to use as an extension. It has become the Art Academy in the Woods. Other schools and structures of the Fraser School District are the Thomas Dooley School/Early Childhood Center, Ralph Waldo Emerson Elementary, and Walt Disney Elementary. Pictured is the former Fraser High School, which became the Howard C. Richards Junior High School.

In 1970, Fraser High School was built. The school system of Fraser had come a long way from the 1864 St. John Lutheran School, at which all the different grades were in the same classroom, and the teacher taught the first through eighth grades.

Around November 1852, the first church of Fraser began when German Lutherans founded the Lutheran church, popularly called the Buffalo Church, or St. John Lutheran Church of Clinton (Township). It was built one quarter mile south of Fifteen Mile Road, and on the west side of Utica Road. A cemetery for the church was on Utica Road by the railroad tracks until the 1920s, when the graves were relocated so the land could be used as a coal yard.

The parsonage for the Lutheran church, pictured here, was to the south of the church, which is visible to the left. The Buffalo Church helped draw enough people to the area to support a general store in 1855.

In 1864, 28 families of the Buffalo Lutheran Church formed the St. John Lutheran Church. They acquired Pastor H. Lembke of Manistee to get them started. Their first wood church, on Fourteen Mile and Utica Roads, cost $3,000. They soon outgrew this church, which was moved to Utica Road where it became Schneider Hardware. A new frame church was built on March 3, 1867. The main builder was Gotthold Hemme. The steeple measured 110 feet, the highest structure in the area. On the inside were fresco drawings and a resurrection mural by artist F.W. Wehle of Milwaukee adorned the altar. Pictured below are St. John schoolchildren.

On Christmas Day 1884, St. John Lutheran Church caught on fire at 1:30 a.m., after the previous evening's candlelight Christmas Eve services. After being awakened by hail-like sounds caused by the fire, parishioners raced out into the snow and tried to fight the fire to no avail. A few men managed to save the communion vessels, linens, and Bible, but the rest of the church was a total loss. The congregation built another church, which survives to this day. The interior of the St. John Lutheran Church is shown below as it looked in the 1950s.

The next St. John Lutheran Church was built on the southwest corner of Fourteen Mile and Utica Roads in 1885, the same year that the first St. John Lutheran School was built. In 1921, another fire burned the church when it was struck by lightning. This time, the church was not a total loss. The interior of the church was ruined by the thunderbolt, but the outer walls remained intact. Since this was the church's second fire, there was consternation voiced by the pastor about the message God was sending to the congregation. Nevertheless, this church served the community until 1986, over 100 years. The previous church became a lighting warehouse, and the cornerstone from the old church is in a pillar at the back of the newest church (pictured). Other features of the new church include a cathedral ceiling, stained-glass windows, and an organ with 2,333 pipes.

St. John Lutheran Church has come a long way since it held services at the Gratiot Drive-in (pictured) in 1954. The drive-in was one of many places the church met over the years while awaiting a permanent structure.

The St. John Lutheran Church is pictured during the 1960s when Dr. Edwin C. Weber was the pastor. Dr. Weber headed the church from 1944 to 1973 and was the one who convinced the congregation to offer their old school building to the library. The library was named the E.C. Weber Fraser Public Library in honor of his service to the community.

The churches of Fraser, like those in many other hamlets and villages, would meet wherever they could find a building. The Zion Evangelical Church first met in Steffens Hall, shown in 1895. The Zion Evangelical and Reformed Church had its start in February 1896 when Reverend P. Haass organized the small congregation, which was first known as the Zion Evangelical Congregation. The congregation had about 30 families at the start and Charles Steffens had recently built the pictured large store building on the corner of Utica and 14 Mile Roads. A second story was built into a hall that came to be known as Steffens's Hall. Steffens acquired a hundred chairs for the hall and allowed the new church to use it for its meetings.

The Zion church had many members by the time the congregation took a trip together to a religious rally in Petoskey. One of the oldest couples to make the trip were Mr. and Mrs. Walter Steffens, pictured in the group above. At left, pictured in 1916, is Pastor John Neumann. As time passed, the church became the Zion United Church of Christ. On September 10, 1972, the 300 members of the church merged with the Grace Church of 2353 East Grand Boulevard in Detroit and became the Zion-Grace United Church of Christ. The Grace Church sold its building to an Assemblies of God congregation. The Grace Church had been without a regular minister for two years, and the merger helped strengthen both churches.

In 1900, the German Evangelical Church congregation decided to build a church. They purchased an acre on Utica Road and Charles Steffens donated most of the material necessary for building the frame building. Other parishioners donated additional materials as well as labor. For many years, the church was referred to as the "Steffens Church." It was dedicated on September 1, 1901, and referred to as "the Chapel of Fraser" by other congregations. The adjoining house was used as a parsonage for Rev. J. Neumann, who served from 1909 until 1917. He was the longest-serving minister for many years. The Board of National Missions began giving financial support to the congregation in 1927. This allowed the congregation to keep regular ministers more consistently and make other improvements, such as digging a basement in 1928, as well as other repairs. A rededication was held on November 4, 1928.

1993

Our Lady Queen of All Saints Catholic Mission was established in Fraser in June 1954 with parishioners from Sacred Heart of Roseville. On September 1, 1954, they began a regular Mass schedule in the Fraser High School auditorium. Soon a cinder block building at 31200 Utica Road (pictured below) became available for purchase from the estate of Anthony Delise, and the congregation moved there. A rectory was built at 31700 Cyril Avenue in 1958, followed by an educational center across the street in 1960 on farmland acquired from George Van Marcke. Groundbreaking for the new church adjacent to the educational center took place in 1966, and the new church was dedicated in March 1967.

Seven

CLUBS AND ORGANIZATIONS

Like so many communities in America, Fraser residents enjoyed taking time out of their busy schedules for recreational pleasures. Sometimes their activities, like hunting, fishing, quilting, and sewing, enhanced their lives with sustenance, warmth, and beautiful clothing. Engaging in sports was also a common pastime for Fraser residents. It had been the national pastime for over 50 years when the Fraser Ball Club was captured in this 1908 photograph. Going out to watch the games was also a part of the community's social scene.

In 1988, Fraser city officials approved a 28-member volunteer fire force proposed by public safety director Ron Wolber. The volunteers were to man the station for eight hours per week and were paid $4 an hour for that time and $8 an hour while fighting a fire. Retired fire sergeant John Sommerville served as director of the volunteer force. Sommerville, who retired from the department in 1987 after 25 years of service, was a member of the original volunteer force in 1960. Volunteers were covered by workers' compensation insurance. The city's insurance cost for the volunteers was less than $1,000 per year. The volunteer firefighters' wages were derived from the budget by delaying the purchase of new portable radios and by not hiring extra personnel for the records department. Fraser firemen pictured in this June 1940 photograph are, from left to right, (first row) Fred Endres, Carl Glatz, Leonard Miesel, William Ward, Ben Reif, and Ed Endres; (second row) Walter Seifferlein, Lowell Steffens, Herman Jacobs, Willard Steffens, Carl Heisner, Omer Elliott, and Harold Skubick. Not pictured is Louis Gideon.

The organizational statement of the Fraser Veterans of Foreign Wars (VFW) Post No. 6691 describes the club as "a fraternal, patriotic, historical, and educational organization; its purpose is to preserve and strengthen comradeship among its members; to assist worthy comrades; to perpetuate the memory and history of the dead and to assist their widows and orphans; to maintain true allegiance to the government of the United States of America and fidelity to its constitution and laws; to foster true patriotism; to maintain and extend the institutions of American freedom; and to preserve and defend the United States from all her enemies." (Both courtesy of Lynn Lyon.)

On April 12, 1946, Fraser VFW Post No. 6691 was formed and installed at the Star Ballroom, now known as the Vintage House. Claude Wood was the first commander for the 52 members. On May 26, 1947, the Ladies Auxiliary was formed. The vets met locally at the Hof Brau Hall, Serement's Bar, Sheppard's Inn, Steffens's Hall, Fraser Lions, the Auction House, the basement of the Fraser Bank, St. John Lutheran Church, and the village town hall until their own VFW hall was completed in 1956. Pictured in December 1947 are Fraser veterans at Serement's Bar (now Bellew's); they were gathered for the reburial of Marvin Nieman.

The Honor Guard Re-Burial of Marvin Nieman
Photographed in December, 1947 at Serement's Bar
Currently: **Mike Foster's Saloon**
Formerly: **The Fraser Hotel (Est. 1859)**

1. Stan Vicks
2. Vern Holcomb
3. Cliff Storks
4. John Schomacher
5. Tom Engel
6. Louis Johnston
7. Ed LaFriniere
8. Richie Collins
9. George Sheppard
10. Skippy Dierlein
11. Bud Schrader
12. Jim Kollmorgen
13. Chuck Collins
14. Arnie Schurig
15. Oliver George
16. Roy Heisner
17. Earl Engel
18. Bob Engel
19. Jim Kelly
20. Mike Kollmorgen
21. Bud Kollmorgen
22. Ralph Kollmorgen
23. Claude Wood

The only Fraser veteran to serve abroad in World War I was Fred Eberlein, the blacksmith (right). Many moneymaking functions for the VFW, like bingo, an ox roast, Circus in the Park, a beef roast picnic, and a log cabin raffle, were held at the Moravian Auction House. On March 12, 1951, a piece of property was purchased from the township for $1. By a vote of 93 to 8 on March 14, 1955, it was exchanged for the land where the post office now sits, and a VFW hall was built. Some of Fraser's many veterans are pictured below marching in the Lions Parade.

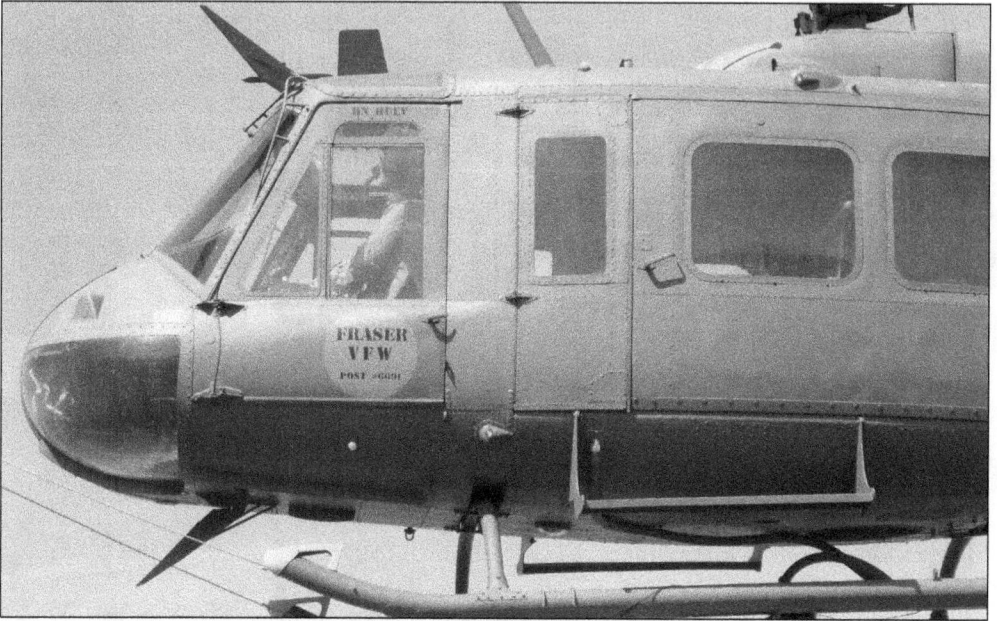

A memorial in the form of a mounted Vietnam War–era UH-1H Iroquois helicopter was installed in front of the VFW Post No. 6691 and was dedicated to all veterans. The motto of the VFW is "Honor the Dead, by Helping the Living." Members teach flag etiquette at the Fraser schools, and also perform flag raisings and Memorial Day services. The VFW was instrumental in sparking interest in the status of the prisoners of war and those missing in action from the Vietnam War. From their fundraisers, they are able to support local programs for DARE, the Kidney Foundation, cancer research, and the National Home for destitute families of deceased veterans. The vets also assist the Salvation Army and social services by collecting food donations, hats, and mittens. Years ago, they served their country; now, they are serving their community. (Both courtesy of Lynn Lyon)

A group of Fraser businessmen formed the Fraser Lions in 1946. The Detroit Gratiot Lions sponsored the club, and on May 13, 1946, Lions International officially chartered the Fraser Lions Club. Membership requirements of Lions International allowed only one person of each profession to join, and membership was limited to 40 people. During the 1960s, the membership limit was increased to 100, and there was a waiting list of businessmen wanting to join. Pictured are the Lions float (above) and the queen's float (below) for the Lions Club parade.

The Lions Parade in July has yielded many colorful floats and beautiful queens. The first dinner and general business meetings were held in the Annex Building behind the old St. John Lutheran Church. The meetings were moved to Sheppard's Inn for approximately one year prior to the building of the St. John Lutheran School.

The Lions Club held its general membership meetings at the school the early 1950s until the mid-1970s. The board meetings were held in the board members' homes, and then moved to the Hof Brau Hall in Fraser. Pictured are the 1955 Lions Club queens.

In the late 1960s, land was purchased for the purpose of building a community building that could be utilized by the Lions Club and other city, school, and civic organizations. When the outside shell of the building was completed, the inside finish work was done by the laborers within the Lions den, and the building was completed in 1974. The picture at left is from the 1955 Lions parade.

The Fraser Lions Club was officially chartered on May 13, 1946. The club started the Fraser Homecoming in the late 1940s as a major fundraiser. The homecoming was held at the Star Ballroom (now the Vintage House), then the Fraser VFW grounds, and finally, Fraser City Park. The Fraser Lions sponsored and helped organize the Sterling Heights Lions Club.

Although not very common in most towns similar in size, the Fraser Lions Club funds an amazingly long and wonderful parade every July. Here, a queen and her court are pictured in this event, which has everything one expects from a parade, like floats representing local businesses, agencies, or other groups; antique automobiles; beautiful women; marching bands; clowns; "freebies" thrown from cars and floats; members representing organizations like the VFW and Shriners; and horses and other animals. Of course, what parade could be complete without the "glad-handing" of local politicians and hopeful politicians? The festivities end with a grand display of fireworks celebrating Fraser as well as America's independence.

Eight

BUSINESS AND INDUSTRY

Fraser began, like most small towns and villages of the 1800s and early 1900s, as a rural, farming community. The first businesses included a blacksmith shop, a sawmill, a general store, a post office, and a bank. Other early businesses included motor sales, the Hof Brau for food and drink, an ice company, a butcher shop, a contracting business, the "Sweet Shop," grocery and hardware stores, and eventually, a bowling alley. In this picture of Ed Deierlein and his horse, Tom, taken on January 9, 1939, it is not determined if he is farming or is at work at the sawmill or blacksmith shop, but it certainly captures the early Fraser landscape. Ed can be seen dancing at the Star Ballroom in Chapter Nine. (Courtesy of Evelyn Imhoff.)

Considered the oldest building in Fraser, this was once the Alexander Fraser Hotel. After that, it was the Measel Hotel, Serement's Bar, and then Mike Foster's Saloon; as of 2013, Ballew's Bar and Grill occupies the building.

This building is located on Utica Road, just north of what were the Grand Trunk Railroad's tracks. The room in the northwest corner of the second floor (shutters open on the window) is purported to have been rented by Thomas Edison. When this property became Mike Foster's Saloon, it was minus the second floor.

The blacksmith shop of Fred Eberlein is considered to be the first business in Fraser, established in 1856. Along with his brother John, Fred Eberlein bought property in Clinton Township, Section 31. Fred's property ran along both sides of Utica Road, from Fourteen Mile Road north to just past Mulvey Road. He also owned land south of Fourteen Mile Road. His blacksmith shop was on the southwest corner of Fourteen Mile and Utica Roads. The two acres west of the shop were sold in 1864 to St. John Lutheran Church of Erin.

The large commercial building of Charles Steffens, also known as Steffens's Hall, which was long a meeting place of Fraser, housed many businesses for many years until the building was razed. Some of these businesses included a pool hall, a Kroger store, a candy shop, a dance hall, and the German Evangelical Church.

In the winter, a sleigh full of logs at the sawmill, complete with workers and their team of horses, was a common sight. Early pioneers never failed to step in if a neighbor was out of firewood or milk for the baby. A different team of sawmill horses, named Ben and Tom, is seen below in 1939 with an unidentified driver and the sawmill in background. (Above, courtesy of Lowell Steffens; below, courtesy of Evelyn Imhoff.)

Steffens's lumber mill was originally called Knorr and Steffens and included a stave and heading mill and an ax handle factory as well as a sawmill. By 1882, the business paid no less than $8,000 in freight to the Grand Trunk Railway and employed 50.

Staves were the side slats used in the construction of barrels. Just about everything that was shipped, whether by ship or rail, was stored in a barrel. Fred Eberlein, William Beaucleac, John Gapt, Charles Knorr, and Charles Steffens owned this stave mill. By 1895, the mill manufactured staves, headings, hardwood lumber, ax handles, whiffletrees, and neck yokes. Later, a feed mill was operated. Charles Steffens also had a thriving coal office at Fourteen Mile and Utica Roads, pictured in the background below.

As Fraser prospered, new businesses provided competition for the more established ones. Pictured is Fraser Lumber in the 1950s, at a time when Steffens Lumber Mill, with its own sawmill, had been established for over 70 years.

Once the railroad tracks were laid in 1849 and a stagecoach began a regular route down Utica Road in 1850, a small settlement began to grow around the present-day Fraser area. In 1855, the Buffalo Church helped draw enough people to the area to support a general store. The general store Schott's Grocery Store evolved into the oldest extant one; it is found on East Fourteen Mile Road between Garfield and Utica Roads. Before the Schott family took over the original general store on Utica Road, the proprietor was David McPherson, a merchant who had moved to the area from the island of Jamaica. As the post office was located in the general store, it also became the place where the stagecoach stopped to let off and take on passengers. This stop was at the area of Fourteen Mile and Utica Roads that became known as McPhersonville. David and his wife, Agnes, owned some land on Mulvey Road also.

101

The c. 1885–1903 view of the Charles Klein General Store below shows the "Post Office of Fraser" sign. This picture was from Karen Held, daughter of Florence Schott Meier, who was the daughter of Bertha Klein Schott, who was married to Fred Schott. Bertha Klein's mother was Wilhemina Meier Klein, who was married to Charles Klein. (Both courtesy of Kenny Klein.)

In early days, it was common to have a post office in a local business, and in most cases, the proprietor of the business would serve as the postmaster. In Fraser, the store that housed the post office served as a central point for the stagecoach to come and go with passengers and mail. Oftentimes, a town was named after the postmaster, and census and postal records of 1860 reflect that the settlement at Fourteen Mile Road near Utica Road was called McPhersonville, named after Jamaican West Indian David McPherson, the first postmaster. He held that post until 1863, when the community's name was changed back to Fraser. Frederick Leerisch then became postmaster. Around the time of McPherson's death, Alexander Fraser was establishing the village of Fraser adjacent to the train depot. The post office was moved to Fraser Hotel or to a grocery store. Postal documents show that the post office was moved in 1863 to a location "perhaps on Depot Road," and it remained there for five years. In 1868, it moved again to Herman Knorr's Grocery. Other early postmasters who worked out of the store included Frederick C. Kollmorgen, as well as William Buckman in 1881, Charles Steffens in 1882, and Charles Klein in 1893. The Fraser Post Office building in the 1930s (pictured) was on Utica Road, between Schott's Grocery Store and Schneider Hardware.

In 1923, there was a threat that the Fraser Post Office would be moved from the town. To prevent this, Fred Schott had a small post office building constructed next to his market. Fifteen years later, in May 1938, Schott's daughter Florence became the postmistress until 1942. Under her supervision, the service quickly advanced to a third-class post office, officially designated on July 7, 1939. Dorothy (née Seiferlein) Ward was appointed in 1951 and served until 1970. Later postmasters were Clarence T. Pokriefka in 1971 and then Maurice DiPasquali in 1978. Schott's Grocery Store was in business in the form of a general store as far back as the mid-1800s. Alfred Schott managed the store for his father, Frederick, during the 1940s and until Fred Schott's death in 1951. Alfred moved the store to its current location at 16655 Fourteen Mile Road, known as the Steffens Block. (Courtesy of Dorothy Steffens Eberlein.)

This is a view of the Fraser Bank, along with the Fraser Motor Sales Garage Building, in 1930. To get the bank started, George Steffens and Henry Bohn approached businessmen and asked for a minimum investment of $1,000 from each person. In half a day, they had collected $20,000 capital, enough to start the bank. Bohn became the bank's cashier, with Charles Burr of Royal Oak the first president and Albert Grabow as vice president. Directors included notable local names such as Charles Klein, William Klein, and W.L. Hartsig. The bank was established at the intersection of Utica Road and Townline (now Fourteen Mile) Road on July 11, 1910. The current building (still standing but no longer the State Bank of Fraser) was constructed in 1930 of Bedford limestone with an American eagle perched atop. The interior design included gray Tennessee marble, Botticino marble from Italy, antique Vermont marble, and solid walnut woodwork. This beautiful edifice cost $47,000 to build. Its opening was heralded by 1,500 people. (Above, courtesy of Melvin Kleino.)

Fraser Bank was robbed in May 1929, and the three young thugs made off with $1,180. A shower of bullets rained upon the three hoodlums, as an assistant cashier of the bank and a Macomb County vigilante member fired upon the fleeing bandits. Other citizens, heeding the vigilante alarm, got into cars to pursue the crooks. The two who robbed the bank jumped onto the running board of a waiting coupe as the driver sped away in the direction of Detroit. To date, the three crooks have never been apprehended. In March 1933, Franklin D. Roosevelt closed every American bank, and some never reopened; happily for our citizens, the State Bank of Fraser did so after just a few days of being closed. Depositors lost nothing, which attests to the integrity of those identified with the institution. It was in this year that an addition was built. Attending the opening was Rev. E.C. Weber of St. John Lutheran Church, who officiated. All residents were invited to come.

In the 1950s, as the new Groesbeck Highway became a major thoroughfare of Fraser, new industry moved into the city, adding revenue to the tax base. This helped prompt the decision for Fraser to go from being a village to a city. The businesses pictured here are still prospering in the 21st century.

Steffens Motor Sales, located on Utica Road on the southeast side of the intersection of Fourteen Mile Road, was a major business in Fraser for many years. Some of the principals are pictured here. From left to right are Marvin Steffens, Alan Reindel, Leonard Meisel, Martin Reif, Ralph Kollmorgen, Ed Endres, and Lowell Steffens. (Courtesy of Jack Kollmorgen.)

Fraser Business School operated in the late 1920s and 1930s. Dress codes required male students to wear ties.

At left, owner Ed Puls (left) and employee Rick Sovy stand in front of the Hof Brau's entrance, located on Utica Road. (Both courtesy of Jack Kollmorgen.)

The Ice Man cometh—in the guise of an employee and a boy. The door of the truck above reads "Jack Kollmorgen Ice, Fraser, Mich." Ice was a big business in Macomb County for many years. Jack Kollmorgen is pictured above with his son Tom, and below by himself. (Both courtesy of Jack Kollmorgen.)

The Rosteks were a notable family of Fraser. They owned Rostek Butcher (or Sausage) Shop and Rostek Contractors. Pictured above is the Rostek farm, and below is one of the many vehicles used in their construction company. (Both courtesy of Bonnie Rostek Layman.)

These two views of the Rostek Butcher Shop in the 1950s show the narrow sidewalks, dirt roads, and fuel oil storage tank on the side of the building. The image below also shows a view of North Utica Road up to Park Lane.

Angie's Restaurant was once Schneider Hardware. The knotty-pine paneling and the boy's patterned shirt suggest this picture was taken in the 1940s or 1950s. The Sheppard's Inn was a well-known landmark restaurant in Fraser, as seen in the 1982 photograph below. Before it was the Sheppard's Inn, it was known as Carl's One-Stop. (Above, courtesy of Mildred Reindel.)

Reindel's first hardware store was on the west side of Utica Road. The building was originally the first church of St. John Lutheran. The family's 1908 International Harvester auto is pictured above at left, with, from left to right, Ross J. Axford, C.J. Reindel, and eight-year-old Allen Reindel. Called the Village Hardware Store, it is pictured below during a Utica Road repair project. (Both courtesy of Karen Held and Irwin Reindel.)

C.J. Reindel Hardware, a brick store, is pictured above with Allen (left) and Charlie Reindel in front in 1962, and below from the inside in 1942. Look at all the modern appliances for sale, like a wringer washing machine! (Both courtesy of Mildred Reindel.)

In 1925, C.J. Reindel Hardware established itself permanently at the location and building where it currently stands and flourishes. It is seen above in 1959 at 32916 Utica Road; it looks the same today. Pictured below is the store's float in the 1954 Lions Parade.

Nine

LEISURE AND RECREATION

Over the years, Fraser has seen its share of Lions parades in July and homecoming parades in the autumn. Located in a central part of town and host to church groups, civic meetings, and other social activities, the Hof Brau has long been a part of Fraser's social scene. Pictured are Ed Puls and employee Rick Sovy inside of the Hof Brau. The bar for the Hof Brau was moved from its previous location, and today it is almost 100 years old.

Leisure activities that helped keep Fraser residents active were music (singing, playing instruments, or dancing), art (painting and sculpting), writing, and stamp, coin, or rock collecting. As Americans began to take motor vacations in the 1950s and needed places to stay when on the road, motels grew up around Groesbeck Avenue. (Above, courtesy of Mildred Schott Skubick.)

This 1960s postcard of the Flamingo Motel on Groesbeck Highway illustrates the marketing of the era, when motorists began using the automobile to travel on vacations. (Courtesy of Eric Gala.)

One of the first buildings of Fraser was Charles Prieh's Beer Hall and Bowling Alley, which provided recreation for Fraser residents for many years.

Nothing beat dancing at the Star Ballroom, such as on this night on May 25, 1941. Dancing has long been a social activity enjoyed by both men and women. Couples could become close swaying to the musical strains of an orchestra, band, or jukebox. The Star Ballroom provided just such a venue for this pleasurable pursuit. Not only was there a lovely dance floor inside the building, but on those glorious summer nights, couples could be seen dancing outside under the stars, thus the name. Above, a celebration of "outdoor gardens," is pictured on May 25, 1941. According to the caption on the back, this is "Most all Fraser Folks." The people that can be identified include William Starkey (fourth from the left), and from the middle, from right to left, Bill Hallendy, Betty Kelly (dark dress, anklets, and white shoes), Jimmy Rose, Dawn Eberlein, Eddie Graham, Beatrice Opal, Leban Myers, Josephine Rose, Margaret Guy, Alger Boening, Phyllis Nelson, Emma Gregg, and Skippy Deierlein. The owner and submitter of the photograph below, Albert Grambo, is standing by the jukebox. Among the couples pictured are Mare Sieger and Jean Campbell, Ruth Faulmann and Charles Skubick, and Emma Gregg and Skip Deierlein. (Above, courtesy of H.M. Sherer; below, courtesy of Albert Grambo.)

Fraser was no different than other communities near the Motor City. Auto repair remained a favored hobby and was perhaps more popular at that time than today. Fraser had a baseball team known as, strangely enough, the Fraser Baseball Team. They played teams in the area from about 1920 to 1930. The players pictured below are, from left to right, (first row) five unidentified, Harold Mellman, and unidentified; (second row) Art Schneider, Carl Heisner, William Glatz, unidentified, Adolph "Windy" Eberlein, and Wilfred Mellman. (Below, courtesy of Dorothy Steffens Eberlein.)

In the Fraser Lions Homecoming Parade of July 20, 1955, the C.J. Reindel Hardware float passes in front of C.J. Reindel Hardware, above. Pictured below is the Hof Brau float in the 1939 parade. The float looked like a typical scene in the local pub with someone at a piano and customers at a table, possibly drinking Altes beer. (Above, courtesy of Audrey DeFauw; below, courtesy of Jack Kollmorgen.)

Inside the Fraser Hof Brau on Utica Road, bartender Jack Kollmorgen can be seen serving five of his customers. Augusta Heisner is second from the left on the barstools. The outside of the Hof Brau was a gathering place for Fraser's finest. (Courtesy of Jack Kollmorgen.)

The "pet parade" at the Fraser Park (later Steffens Park) was a great way to involve the children of the community in a fun activity! From left to right are Walter Steffens, Pam Young, Nancy Young, two unidentified, and LeRoy Call on the tractor. In 1940, Fraser Park was dedicated by a village council proclamation with trees planted to commemorate the event. Part of the land that makes up the Walter C. Steffens Park was part of the Boeckenhauer Farm, which extended from the railroad tracks west to Utica Road. The remainder of the park was acquired by the city under the Scavenger Tax Act, which allowed a city to purchase land that was delinquent in taxes from the state of Michigan. In 1963, the park was renamed to honor Walter C. Steffens, who was very much a part of our history, with a monument built to mark the occasion. Steffens was the village president when the land had been purchased for Fraser Park. He is seen at left in his wedding picture with his wife Carolyn. (Above, courtesy of Angie Call.)

Pictured are Fraser men posing with the catch of the day. Here is a hobby that serves a dual purpose—food and fun! Pictured above are, from left to right, (first row) Albert Grambo, Fred Eberlein, Charles Kollmorgen, and Fred Schott; (second row) unidentified, Carl Schindewolf, Carl Steffens, Alfred Schott, and unidentified. Below, rabbit hunters display their game against the backdrop of a car and a couple of city buildings. Pictured are Oscar Seifferlein and Vince Schultz. (Both courtesy of Jack Kollmorgen.)

At left, three Fraser hunters show their prowess by shooting from the roof of an outhouse. Below, movie star Mickey Rooney was in Fraser on February 10, 1940, on a train stop along the route to Port Huron, Michigan, where the film *Young Thomas Edison* premiered that day. Rooney arrived on wood-burning locomotive *Old Sam Hill*, on which young Tom Edison printed, edited, and published the *Grand Trunk Herald*, the first newspaper published on a train. Rooney's first stop was in Fraser, where station agent. J.J. Longnecker faced the task of controlling a crowd estimated between 4,000 and 5,000 people, many of them children. Two bands played for the entertainment of those waiting. Other notables riding with Rooney on the train that day were Mina Edison Hughes, Edison's widow; Gov. Luren Dickinson; and Edsel Ford. It was in Fraser where Edison suffered the ear injury that contributed to his deafness in later life. According to legend, Edison almost missed the train, but the conductor pulled him aboard by the ears. (Below, courtesy of Jenny Heiman.)

ABOUT THE AUTHORS

James Chamberlin is a 40-year resident of Fraser and retired from IBM as a system analyst. After retirement, he contracted back for 10 years as project manager for IBM. He is currently the Men's Club secretary, St. Vincent de Paul secretary-treasurer, and a member of the Fraser Goodfellows and American Legion. His education includes a bachelor's of business administration, a master's of science in management, and a certificate in project management.

Linda S. Champion received her bachelor's degree from Oakland University and her master's degree from Wayne State University in Detroit. She worked for the Macomb County Library in Clinton Township for almost 27 years before retirement. She was the editor for Douglas Casamer's nonfiction Civil War book *The History of the Michigan 22nd Infantry Regiment and the Men Who Served* (2006). Linda was awarded many NACo (National Association of Counties) awards, including NACo's special award for Best in Library category. Linda currently writes articles for *Strawberry Preserves*, the Fraser history newsletter.

Jan Dolland was born and raised in Fraser, and her family history in the area goes back to 1875. She is retired with a bachelor's degree in home economics and is a lecturer on quilts, a chocolatier, and a teacher of cooking classes.

Nancy Ehrke was named Volunteer of the Year for Fraser at a Macomb County Commission meeting in 2012. She has a bachelor's degree in business administration from Northwood University and was community development supervisor for the city of Mount Clemens. She is a member of the Fraser Historical Commission, president of the Fraser Library Board, vice president of the Fraser Planning Commission, member of the Goodfellows, and coordinator of the Fraser Book Committee.

Alan Naldrett was a charter member of the Macomb County Historical Commission and has been on the Chesterfield Township Board of Trustees for 12 years. He has written two other local history books and has written articles for the New York *Village Voice*, the Macomb County history website, and many local publications. He is formerly the editor of the Baker College of Auburn Hills newsletter and currently does the Baker College alumni newsletter. For over 10 years he has been an academic librarian as well as an archivist, and has two master's degrees.

Gary Nizio has been a Fraser area resident for about 45 years, graduated from the Fraser school district, and received a business degree from Macomb College. He especially enjoys history projects, which is why he volunteered for the Fraser History Book Committee.

Marilynn D. Wright has been a Fraser resident for over 50 years and has been the chairwoman of the Fraser Historical Commission for 12 years. She is the trustee of the Fraser Historical Society and Fraser General Election precinct chairwoman. A retired auditor, she writes for the Fraser history newsletter, *Strawberry Preserves*, and for the St. John Lutheran Church newsletter; she also helps to schedule events at her church.

www.ingramcontent.com/pod-product-compliance
Lightning Source LLC
Chambersburg PA
CBHW050623110426
42813CB00007B/1705